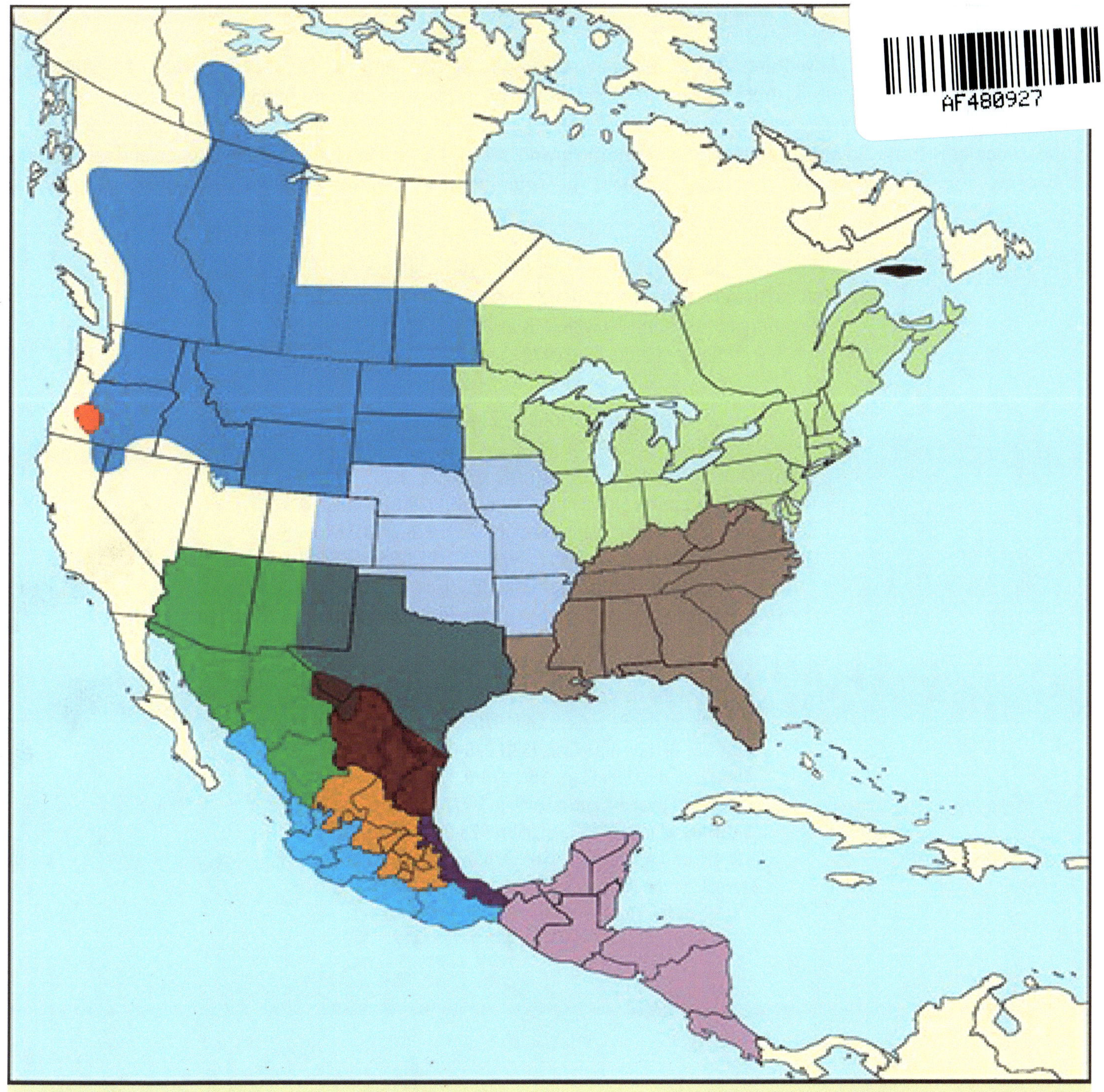

BLUE North-western white tailed deer **GREEN** North-eastern white tailed

Zig Misiak: Author   Jennifer Bettio: Illustrator

Contributor: Raymond R. Skye, Tuscarora/Seneca, Grand River Six Nations Territory

Educational consultant: Shaylyn Misiak, ECE, BEd, BA (hons.), OCT

Revised 2022, ISBN 978-0-9950128-6-8

Other publications by Zig Misiak

FIRST NATIONS RESOURCE COLLECTION, ISBN 978-0-9811880-2-7
WAMPUM: The Story of Shaylyn the Clam, ISBN-978-0-9811880-8-9
WAR of 1812: Highlighting Native Nations, ISBN 978-0-9811880-5-8
WAR of 1812: Western Hooves of Thunder, ISBN 978-0-9811880-3-4
TONTO: The Man in Front of the Mask, ISBN 978-0-9811880-6-5
4 in 1 LEARNING: French & English, ISBN 978-0-9950128-0-6
ABC's Colouring Book, ISBN 978-0-9950128-9-9
1-2-3's, Shapes & Colours Colouring Book, ISBN 978-1-7771417-0-7
ASHER: of the Heron Clan, ISBN 978-0-9950128-3-7
COLTON: of the Bear Clan, ISBN 978-8-9950128-2-0
CRISTINE: of the Snipe Clan, ISBN 978-0-9950128-7-5
DARYL: of the Deer Clan, ISBN 978-0-9950128-6-8
LUKE: of the Eel Clan, ISBN 978-1-7771417-7-6
MEAGHAN: of the Hawk Clan, ISBN 978-0-9950128-8-2
RYAN: of the Wolf Clan, ISBN 978-0-9950128-5-1
STANLEY: of the Beaver Clan, ISBN 978-1-7771417-8-3
TYLER: of the Turtle Clan, ISBN 978-0-9950128-1-3
POLISH Heritage Guide, ISBN 978-1-7771417-5-2

www.canadianauthoreducation.com

About Clans

All **First Nations, Métis and Inuit People**, similar to other nations around the world, have a family system. The First Nations Métis, and Inuit people are interwoven with nature like interdependent fibres in the colourful and mysterious tapestry of life.

Clans existed well before Europeans came to **Turtle Island**, known to many as North America. In the world of the **Haudenosaunee**, also known as the Six Nations or Iroquois, they even existed before the coming of the **Peacemaker**.

The DEER, the main story in this book, is one of the nine (9) Clan animals of the Six Nations. These two introductory pages, plus the supplemental pages at the end of the story, will be informative.

Relax and get ready to enjoy the Deer's adventures in the meadow as well as becoming enlightened about First Nations Clans.

9 Clans of the Haudenosaunee

Of the land	Bear	Wolf	Deer
Of the water	Eel	Beaver	Turtle
Of the air	Heron	Snipe	Hawk

Other examples of First Nations animals and relations.

West Coast Haida

They belong to one of two groups of Clans, the Eagle or the Raven.

Anishinaabe Clans

Bear, Otter, Fish, Eagle, Loon, Crane, Deer.

Mikmaq Spirit Animals

Bear, Lynx, Beaver, Crow, Eagle, Fox, Moose, Wolf.

The Young Man and the Clans

The **Young Man** noticed that there was a lack of support between people, especially when they were grieving. He spoke to the elders saying that all of nature worked in harmony and that humans needed to get back into that harmonious natural rhythm.

He was permitted to unfold his plan. First he had all the elder women of each family find and observe an animal they were drawn too. Over some time the women came back to him with their choices. He assigned those particular animals to each unit giving them that animals name.

He then had all the people gather at the river. There he divided them into two predetermined groups having one half cross to the other side.

Once everyone was settled in, the Young Man explained that the river was like the fire in their lodges that divided the mothers and father sides of the family.

He said, "Let the fire symbolize the division the river created. Let the Clans support and address each other across the fire in the longhouses. During loss the related Clans on the opposite side will console and lend assistance to those in grief."

The **Matriarchal** Clan system was born and created a strong bond amongst the Original Ones, the **Onkwehon:we**, becoming an important part of their lives, then and now.

The Young Man's concept of bringing the people together, as extended families, served them well. They worked together and continued to learn from nature, caring for it as the **Creator** had intended.

The Peacemaker

Sadly, when the Peacemaker arrived, years later, the Clan system was dysfunctional due to constant warfare between the nations. The Peacemaker, a woman named **Jikonsaseh** and **Hayenwah:tha**, re-established the Clans creating a strong foundation for their newly organized **Confederacy** based on the **Great Law of Peace**. He told the Onkwehon:we that from now on they would also be known as the Haudenosaunee, the People Building a Longhouse.

The Stories of Creation, formation of the Clans, the coming of the Peacemaker leading to the existence of the Confederacy are all available in detail in the Six Nations Iroquois Program Teachers Resource Guide . Written by Raymond R. Skye, Tuscarora/Seneca, and collaborators, from the Grand River Six Nations Territory and related Six Nations communities.

Daryl Anthony Misiak
Our Son

* 

Daryl and his sister were both born on a bright sunny spring day in April. Their fur was a light reddish brown dotted with white spots. The spots helped the **fawns** blend in with their surroundings when their mother was away and they were alone. It was camouflage.

The siblings curled themselves up into small balls and snuggled close to their mother **doe.** They could feel and hear her heartbeat. It was very soothing. For now their mother would feed them milk. In four weeks the fawns started eating solid food in addition to milk.

Daryl and his sister could walk within seven hours of birth. It would take a few weeks before they were really stable on their long lanky legs. They enjoyed playing and running in the meadows nearby. Deer are one of the forests most gentle creatures.

During the day their mother purposely stayed some distance away from her babies in order not to draw predators to them. It was only at dawn and dusk, usually, that she would nurture her two fawns by snuggling and feeding them.

Daryl and his sister stopped needing milk, now that three months had passed, and were eating plants on their own. They still looked similar except that Daryl now had two bumps on his head. These were antlers in the process of growing. Only the males grew antlers.

One morning, when their mother left for the day and his sister was still sleeping, Daryl got up and walked out among the trees nearby. He was drawn to a particular tree when he heard the melody of birds tweeting. It was quite pleasant.

He wandered under a young maple tree. Looking up he saw two beautiful **cardinals** perched on either side of a nest. The male was brilliant red and the female was tan with some red.

Daryl listened to the beautiful songbird harmony made by the adults. It was disrupted by squeaking coming from inside the nest where four baby cardinals lay huddled together.

Cardinals mate for life. Each year the female would lay from three to four eggs. Both parents took turns keeping their eggs warm and safe. In about two weeks new babies would hatch. The cardinal parents would then take turns feeding the little ones.

Daryl could have stood there all day watching and listening to this happy family but he got distracted by something else that affected one of his other senses, his sense of smell.

He turned to his right and walked in the direction of this rather unpleasant odour. Peering from behind a tree, Daryl found out where the odour was coming from.

Daryl saw two young **skunks** scampering on top of a log. Black with white stripes from the tips of their noses to the tips of their bushy tails, these little skunks were having a great time playing with one another. Daryl, however, wisely kept his distance.

Skunks are generally night creatures but these young ones, like Daryl, broke some survival rules and decided to come out in daylight anyway. It was quite likely that their mother, unseen, was watching from their den nearby and the little ones were feeling very safe.

Skunks have a great sense of smell and hearing but their vision is rather poor. Daryl was downwind so they did not sense him and did not see him either. Even though these skunks looked small and fragile they had a weapon that was known by every creature in the forest.

Skunks have two pouches of spray in their back end. These small innocent looking young skunks could spray accurately up to three meters. The spray was long lasting and smells like rotten eggs. Daryl walked away quietly in a large circle avoiding them.

Every animal in the forest has some unique way to defend itself against predators. It may be camouflage, speed, safety in numbers, hiding abilities, scent, antlers and other things.

Daryl had already met two critters, the skunks, that used their scent to protect themselves.

Daryl now came face to face with a cute chunky little animal called a **porcupine**. How did it protect itself?

As soon as Daryl was seen by the porcupette it rolled into a ball and made its quills shake. The shaking of the quills, along with the little clicks and hisses he was making with his mouth, warned Daryl, or any would be attacker, that they should be careful and stay away.

Daryl, puzzled, stood still as the porcupette was going through his defensive manoeuvers. The porcupette soon realized that Daryl was not a threat. It stood on its two back legs and comfortably continued to chew on the bark it had pulled off the tree stump earlier.

Porcupines eat a lot of bark, stems, nuts, tubers, seeds, grass, leaves, fruit and buds. Normally nocturnal, they do come out occasionally in the day time to enjoy the sun.

If Daryl had not stopped a few feet away from the porcupette, but moved closer to touch its nose, he would have been unpleasantly surprised getting porcupine quills stuck to his face.

Porcupine quills are quite loose and designed to come out rather easily. They would painfully pierce any exposed part of an attacking animal that touched them.

It was impossible for Daryl absorb all the beauties of nature in one day. Every one of his senses were affected. Seeing, smelling, hearing, and touching his surroundings gave him an energy that he had not experienced before. He was becoming one with nature.

Mother Nature helped create thousands of plant species of different shapes and colours. There were creatures that lived among the branches and leaves of the trees. There were those that lived close to the surface and those that lived underground. Then of course there were many larger and smaller critters that walked on the top of the earth, just like Daryl.

A plant that caught Daryl's attention was the **bunchberry**. These creeping plants create a beautiful lush green blanket growing low and thick on the forest floor. Their flowers produces yummy edible berries.

The Cree people call the bunchberry the kawiscowimin meaning 'gravel inside' because when the berries were chewed the seeds made a crackling sound. These juicy red berries are also eaten by bears, rabbits, and yes, even by deer like Daryl.

Daryl did not have any berries to eat that day. It was just a little too early in the season for the berries to have grown and matured. No doubt Daryl would be back.

Daryl heard the sound of water nearby. He trotted off to investigate. Water was tumbling and bubbling over stones in a creek. The suns rays danced off the ripples. He was thirsty. He bent his front legs, and kneeling he began to lap up some of the cold fresh water.

Daryl heard other sounds in the distance. He stood up and started walking toward them.

Daryl heard giggling coming from the other side of a small mound. He cautiously crept to the top of the mound and peaked around a tree. A young boy saw Daryl and smiled but did not say anything. This First Nations family was in the forest gathering things for their village.

The father was nearby leaning against a tree. He was watching over his family as the mother and two youngsters were picking edible wild mushrooms, berries and pieces of black **flint.** These were all placed into three separate woven baskets that each of them carried.

The mushrooms and berries would be cleaned. Some of the mushrooms, and select berries, would be used for ingredients in medicines and some simply eaten. The flint would be chipped and shaped making sharp arrowheads and tools for cutting and scraping.

Without a word, the mother and her two children stood, picked up their baskets, and they silently meandered along a well worn path leading back to their nearby village. Father followed them. Daryl was sad to see them leave.

Daryl casually, but well hidden behind the shrubs, and trees, walked past the village. He was aware of the sun's position in the sky and that gave him a sense of the time of day. He knew that he needed to be back home soon, before dark.

Daryl almost walked past a reddish-brown mound. He stopped and saw that it was made up of three small animals all curled up together. Their bodies were accented with white highlights around their heads, chests, and tips of their bushy tails. The bottom half of their legs were black. It looked as if they were wearing stockings.

Adult **foxes** usually live alone and generally hunt during the night. These three young red foxes, remaining in a group for now, were tired after playing and were simply taking a well deserved nap. Foxes like to play.

The only thing Daryl saw move was the occasional twitch of their ears and tails and the slight expansion of their chest caused by their breathing.

Red foxes belong to the dog family and there are about thirty species of foxes in the world. Foxes are often called sly or sneaky. They walk on the tips of their toes and when in motion their long sleek bodies make them appear as if they are skulking around. After all, they have to be sly to hunt and to avoid predators.

Daryl, not waking them, quietly walked around the bundle moving deeper into the forest.

Daryl came across the same creek that he drank from earlier. It meandered throughout the forest, in the lowlands, flowing gently in and around the rocks, trees and bushes. Daryl lowered his head and with his tongue started to lap up more of the cool clear water.

Daryl smelled a musky odor but did not know where it came from. The **muskrat** moved as it started to chew on a plant root. It was only then that Daryl saw it. Its brown coat blended in with the sandy soil and it was partially hidden behind a small bulrush.

As Daryl continued to drink, his eyes were slightly elevated watching the muskrat. They can be aggressive. They have sharp front claws for digging and webbed feet for swimming. Muskrats are about the size of a squirrel and look like a cross between a rat and a beaver.

Daryl lowered himself on the soft foliage along the side of the creek and having satisfied his thirst curled up into a little ball. He placed his head on his legs and let his eyes slowly close. He felt safe because his acute sense of smell and hearing would alert him to any danger.

Daryl only snoozed for about ten minutes. He stood up and saw that the muskrat was gone.

For some reason Daryl started to walk backwards moving into a cluster of flowering bushes and shrubs. He looked to his left and his nose came within a few inches of a long green insect that was munching on a leaf.

Its head rotated on an angle looking at Daryl. Suddenly its front legs, having claws, shot out at lightening speed toward Daryl's nose. Daryl was a safe distance away and it was a good thing that Daryl was as big as he was. **Praying mantises** are known to successfully attack small birds, lizards and frogs with their raptorial legs.

Mantises have amazing flexibility being able to move their heads 180 degrees, with some species able to move their heads 300 degrees. Their eyes are large and they have excellent peripheral vision for spotting both prey and predator.

Praying mantises can fly and are generally green or brown. They also could remain absolutely still for long periods and blending in with their surroundings.

Daryl seemed to be hypnotized by this tiny green aggressive creature. The mantis, after his first attempt to attack Daryl, retracted its claws and had not moved since.

Daryl, gazing, blinked a few times and stepped back a couple of feet. He then turned to walk away but glanced over his shoulder, just once, as he left this little angry insect alone.

Daryl finally decided to start heading back to where his mother and sister were. The sun had moved across the sky and began to set in the west. Shadows were becoming darker as fewer sun's rays could penetrate the leaves on the trees.

Daryl trotted for about ten minutes when he spotted an unusual looking animal near a hollowed-out tree stump. This **weasel** was quite low to the ground having rather short legs. It was brown, with a white underbelly, and it was long and thin.

When it saw Daryl the weasel started to move, snake-like, squirming and running in and around the stump. When weasels are threatened, or when they are stalking a prey, they do a hypnotic type of movement that looks like they are dancing.

Weasels thin bodies and short legs allow them to chase and follow their prey into the narrowest of spaces. They are the smallest **carnivore** in the world growing to a peak size of twelve inches.

Daryl stepped a little closer to the weasel but the weasel would not stop jumping around. Daryl's nose twitched as he inhaled an unpleasant scent coming from the weasel. Weasels and skunks are members of the same family and can spray a pungent liquid just like skunks. Daryl's instincts made him quickly move back to a safer distance.

Daryl had enough of this weasel and he started walking a little quicker in the direction of his own home. Daryl felt more grownup and seemed to be pleased with his adventures today.

Daryl arrived home safe and sound. His mother was there to greet him. She was standing tall, and alert, ears perked, always listening for anything that might endanger her family.

Daryl walked over to his mother. Both of their short tails started to wag. Expressing their love for one another they gently touched noses.

Daryl's sister was out of sight but Daryl knew she was hidden nearby curled up in a little ball and sleeping. He would soon join her but first he wanted to go see his father.

Normally the **bucks** do not stay with the does and fawns but live in a herd of just bucks. It is only during mating season that the bucks would mingle with the doe and fawn herd.

Daryl was a young buck in the making and he was pleased to see his father among them. He walked over to his father and stood near him looking in the same direction his father was.

His father was tall and majestic wearing a beautiful crown of antlers. Daryl would soon be just like his father. Someday, when Daryl had his own fawns, they would admire him as well.

Key Vocabulary

Buck: This is a male deer. Only bucks have antlers. White tailed deer are the smallest deer in North America.

Bunchberry: It is the unofficial flower of Canada. Their berries can be made into jams.

Cardinal: Named after Roman Catholic Cardinals who wear bright red garments. It is said that 'when cardinals appear angels are near'.

Carnivore: Is a flesh eating animal, such as the weasel, wolf, bobcat, seal, and polar bear.

Clans: Traditionally, not always, Clans are a group of people related by a blood-line. Usually, in this part of the world, through the women. For example, in the Haudenosaunee culture an individual would have their own personal name, belonging to the Wolf Clan of the Mohawk Nation.

Confederacy: The union of the original Five Nations under the Great Law of Peace as composed and implemented by the Peacemaker, Hayenwah:tha and Jikonsaseh. It re-established the Clan system and the Nations councils.

Creator: As it is with many other nations around the world there is a Creator of all things. All First Nations, Inuit and Métis have a Creator in their stories related to the 'Beginning Times'.

Doe: This is the female deer. They do not have antlers. Deer have the same number of teeth as humans.

Fawn: A doe stays with its mother for a couple of years but a buck, the male, will leave after one year.

First Nations, Métis and Inuit People: First Nations were once referred to as 'Indians' in Canada and still are in the United States. First Nations are the 'Original People' from this part of the world. The Métis are people of mixed blood, First Nations and Euro-American. Inuit, living in northern Canada, parts of Greenland and Alaska, are not First Nations but are also 'Original People'. Indigenous, Aboriginal and Native are all words that are used interchangeably when referring to the three groupings of people. The word 'Indian' is more acceptable when used in a historic context.

Flint: A hard yet brittle sedimentary rock. It was very important to First Nations people as it was used for hunting tools, cutting and scraping tools as well as for starting fires. Can be dark grey, black, green, white or brown in colour.

Great Law of Peace: It is an actual living and breathing oral, then later written, document outlining guidelines where reason, moderation and careful discussion were informed and influenced by past events, the current situation, and the possible impact on seven generations into the future. (www.canadianauthoreducation.com)

Haudenosaunee: In the Onondaga language this means the People of the Longhouse or the Longhouse Builders. The original Five Nations Confederacy consisted of the Mohawk, Seneca, Onondaga, Oneida and Cayuga People.

Key Vocabulary

Hayenwah:tha: He was born Onondaga. He suffered greatly before coming into contact with the Peacemaker. He was crucial in assisting the Peacemaker with spreading the peace among the nations and establishing the 'Great Law of Peace'.

Jikonsaseh: The Peacemaker converted her from evil and she then became one of his biggest supporters spreading the 'Good Word'. She is sometimes referred to as the original Clan Mother.

Matriarchal: A system based on female lineage wherein women had great influence, control and leadership in all aspects of a particular society.

Muskrat: Named so because they look like rats and have a musky smell. Babies are called kits.

Onkwehon:we: In the Mohawk language this is translated as the 'Original People' or the 'First Ones'. Inuit also refer to themselves in this way.

Peacemaker: He was a Wyandot who, with the help of others, brought the original Five Nations of the Haudenosaunee together in peace. The Great Law of Peace evolved and the Haudenosaunee Confederacy was born.

Porcupine: A baby is called a porcupette. Porcupine quills do not shoot out but do come out easily when touched.

Praying Mantis: Over 2000 species world wide. So called because they look like they are praying.

Red Fox: Female called a vixen, male a dog-fox and babies cubs. A group is called a skulk.

Skunk: The white stripes of a skunk are meant to be recognized by predators. They know how bad skunks spray is.

Turtle Island: In the Haudenosaunee creation story, a woman, Sky Woman, fell from the sky landing on a sea turtle. Over a long period of time many other land masses were formed on earth. North America is a part of Turtle Island.

Young Man: Inspired by the Creator, this man presented a plan to his people from which the Clan system was born.

Weasel: A group of weasels are called a boogle, confusion, gang, or pack. Young ones are called kits.

Deer Clan

Oskennon:ton Ota:ra

Pronounced: Oh-sgeh-no-doh Odah-rah

Fair, perceptive, athletic, good leaders, faithful

People of the Deer Clan are regarded as being good natured, loyal and very perceptive. Dedication, determination and good leadership skills are other traits that serve them well. Centuries ago a man known as the Peacemaker was instrumental in establishing peace among five warring Iroquois nations. His divine guidance helped the five nations form a great confederation known as the Great Law of Peace. The Peacemaker proclaimed that the deer would be a vital part of Iroquois survival and tradition. The Deer Clan gained notable status among the Iroquois nations for this reason.

Deer Clan people are steadfast when it comes to protecting and upholding their sacred customs. When an Iroquois hunter takes down a deer he will offer thanks to the animals spirit for providing sustenance to the people. Venison is not only a favourite food of the Iroquois, but also serves as an integral part of their ceremonies right to this day. Traditional buckskin clothing is still made from the hide. The antlers of the deer are placed upon the headdress of an Iroquois chief. This denotes his status as a leader of his clan and nation. The Deer Clan holds great respect for the animal they deem as being the symbol of their clan family.

Words by: Awedodyoh, Raymond R. Skye

Tuscarora * Seneca

Grand River Six Nations Territory

www.canadianauthoreducation.com

Questions & Answers

1. **What was the main purpose of the Clan?**

To create family units that would help one another through daily living but mainly for consoling during times of grief.

2. **Who played a key part in developing the Clans and how?**

The Young Man presented the idea first to the elders then he was allowed to speak to the people.

3. **How did the Clan animals help the people develop character?**

They were examples of co-operation and coexistence with nature.

4. **Who were the key players in the Clan structure and what roles did they play?**

The women, caretakers of life, watched and selected the animals they related to.

5. **How would Clan members take care of one another?**

Support one another every day. Help each other by sharing the necessities of life. Remind one another to be thankful to the Creator and observe the ceremonies.

6. **How did the Clan structure help build a sense of community?**

It created family relations that were obligated to help one another. Heron Clan helped Heron Clan within a particular nation but did not exclude interacting with other Clans in other nations.

7. **What do you think a person would do if they saw one of their Clan members being bullied or struggling to learn something?**

They would help them by trying to create a peaceful solution failing that by removing them from

		Hawk	Bear	Wolf	Turtle	Heron	Snipe	Deer	Beaver	Eel
Mohawk			X	X	X					
Seneca		X	X	X	X	X	X	X	X	
Oneida			X	X	X					
Onondaga		X	X	X	X	X	X	X	X	X
Cayuga			X	X	X	X	X			
Tuscarora			X	X	X		X	X	X	X

* Shaded area depicts the **Clans common** to all the Haudenosaunee (Six Nations) People

Can you identify the 9 Clan animals prints?

The 9 Clan animals prints identified.

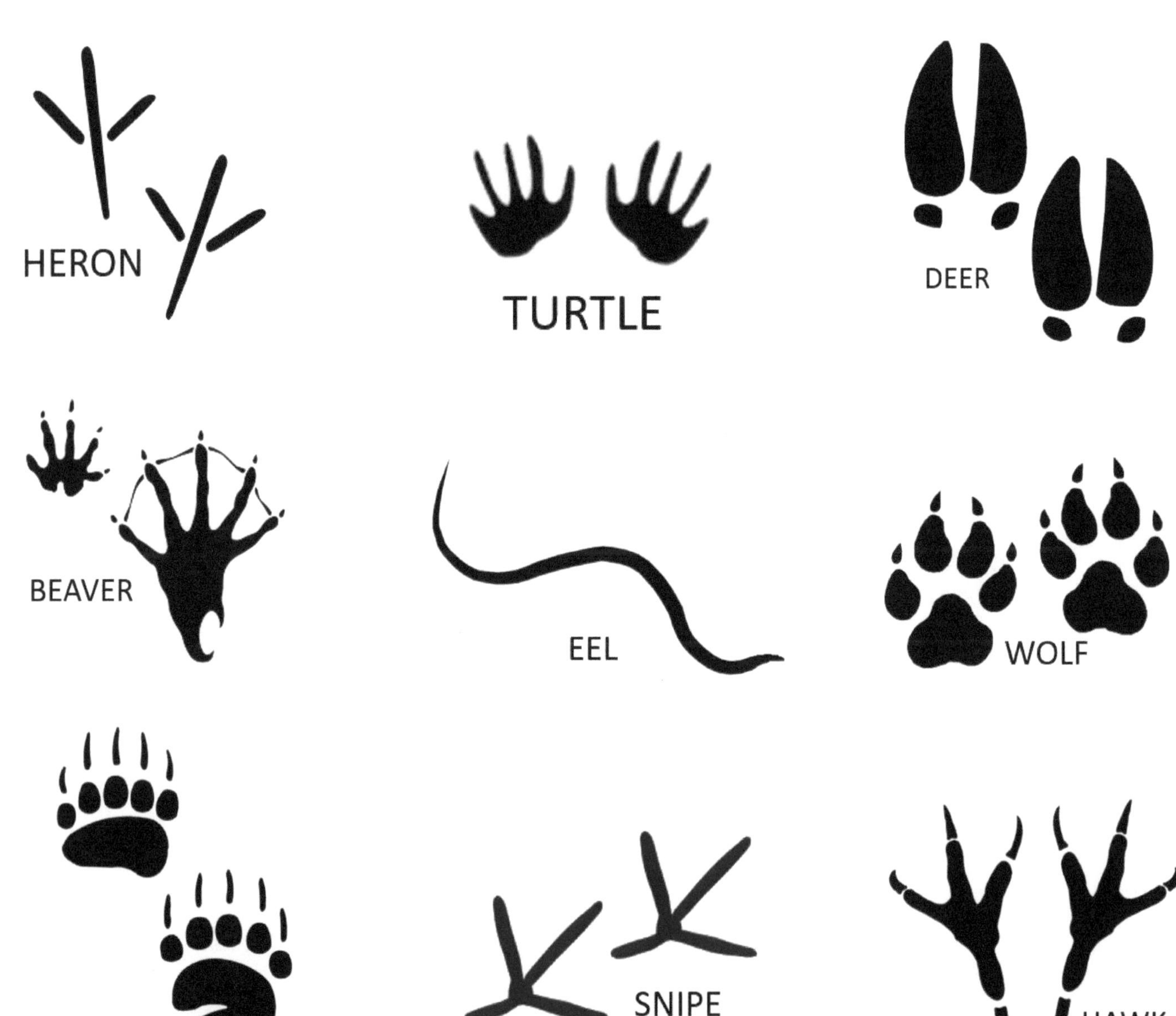

Colouring Activity

Artist's Name:

Zig Misiak is a highly respected, award-winning Canadian author of First Nations books and educational resources. As a child, often on his own, Zig became very curious about the children "across the bridge" at the nearby residential school in Brantford, Ontario. Then, as an adult, he embraced and cultivated interest and enduring relationships with his neighbours and friends, the Haudenosaunee, the Grand River Six Nations People.

Queen Elizabeth II Diamond Jubilee Medal
Sovereign's Medal
Lieutenant Governor's Ontario Heritage Award for Lifetime Achievement
Polish Army Gold Medal - 1st Degree
Canadian Polish Congress Award of Merit
Polish Combatants' Bronze Cross
Shining Star Award
George and Olive Seibel Award
Inductee: Ancaster High School Hall of Distinction
Canadian Aboriginal Veterans Association Medallion

Zig Misiak, became a well-known historical re-enactor who has travelled thousands of miles across Eastern Canada and the United States, participating in the re-enacting of major historical events from the French and Indian Wars, American Revolution, to the War of 1812. He also served in the Canadian Army, Royal Hamilton Light Infantry.

He is now recognized as an authority and a legend for his knowledge, understanding, and commitment to authenticity, as well as the strong friendships he has developed. He has studied and travelled to the very places he has written about in his many books. Zig has a deep love and respect for Indigenous People, recognizing that in spite of the many difficult challenges they have faced, they have remained true to their treaties. As Zig says, **"We must know them."**

Jennifer Bettio, born and raised in Guelph Ontario, is an arts and photography graduate of Sheridan College. With support of her parents she pursued her interests in the arts field that has brought her great success. She does commissioned paintings, art, graphics and design, advertising, illustrations and unique photography. Her French Canadian Métis background, allows her to exhibit a unique First Nations and Métis style of art.

www.ingramcontent.com/pod-product-compliance
Lightning Source LLC
Chambersburg PA
CBHW041950140726
48006CB00004BA/1031
9798844350382